# SPORTING EVENTS

**FROM BASEBALL TO SKATEBOARDING**

by Gabriel Kaufman

Consultant: Paul F. Johnston, Washington, D.C.

BEARPORT
PUBLISHING COMPANY, INC.

New York, New York

Credits:
Cover illustration, Michelle Barbera; soccer ball, TL-Software/istockphoto; football, Dusty Cline/ istockphoto; 4, FAYEZ NURELDINE/AFP/Getty Images; 5(T), Elsa/Getty Images; 5(B), Nick Wass/Getty Images; 6, Nick Laham/Getty Images; 7(T), Ezra Shaw/Getty Images; 7(B), Brian Bahr/Getty Images; 8, Jim McIsaac/Getty Images; 9(T), Nathaniel S. Butler/NBAE via Getty Images; 9(B), WILLIAM PHILPOTT/AFP/Getty Images; 10, Andy Lyons/Getty Images; 11(T), Scott McDermott/Corbis; 11(B), Sean Garnsworthy/Getty Images; 12, JAVIER SORIANO/ AFP/Getty Images; 13(T), Wally McNamee/Corbis; 13(B), Doug Pensinger/ALLSPORT/Getty Images; 14, Bettmann/Corbis; 15(T), Mike Powell/Allsport/Getty Images; 15(B), TIMOTHY A. CLARY/AFP/Getty Images; 16, New York Times Co./Getty Images; 17(T), Jamie McDonald/Getty Images for Laureus; 17(B), Matthew Stockman/Getty Images; 18, Neal Preston/Corbis; 19(T), Marc Serota/Reuters/Corbis; 19(B), Jed Jacobsohn/Getty Images; 20, Bettmann/Corbis; 21(T), Donald Miralle/Getty Images; 21(B), Brian Bahr/Getty Images; 22, Stapleton Collection/Corbis; 23(T), Tim de Waele/Corbis; 23(B), Victor Decolongon/Getty Images; 24, Reuters/Corbis; 25(T), Peter Sterling/Taxi/Getty Images; 25(B), Olivier Renck/Aurora/Getty Images.

Design and production by Dawn Beard Creative and Octavo Design and Production, Inc.

*Library of Congress Cataloging-in-Publication Data*

Kaufman, Gabriel.
  Sporting events : from baseball to skateboarding / by Gabriel Kaufman.
    p. cm. — (Which came first?)
  Includes bibliographical references and index.
  ISBN 1-59716-132-2 (library binding) — ISBN 1-59716-139-X (pbk.)
  1. Sports—Miscellanea—Juvenile literature. I. Title. II. Series.

GV707.K38 2006
796—dc22
                    2005031644

For more information, write to Bearport Publishing Company, Inc., 101 Fifth Avenue, Suite 6R, New York, New York 10003. Printed in the United States of America.

1 2 3 4 5 6 7 8 9 10

# Contents

**6**

**9**

**17**

**19**

**23**

| | |
|---|---|
| Introduction | 4 |
| Football or Soccer | 5 |
| Baseball or Softball | 7 |
| Basketball or Golf | 9 |
| Tennis or Volleyball | 11 |
| Ice Hockey or Lacrosse | 13 |
| Track and Field or Swimming | 15 |
| Skateboarding or Figure Skating | 17 |
| Super Bowl or World Series | 19 |
| Olympics or X-Games | 21 |
| Tour de France or World Cup | 23 |
| Which Comes Next? | 25 |
| Scorecard | 26 |
| Bonus Questions | 27 |
| Just the Facts | 28 |
| The History of Sporting Events | 29 |
| Glossary | 30 |
| Bibliography | 31 |
| Read More | 31 |
| Learn More Online | 31 |
| Index | 32 |
| About the Author | 32 |

# Introduction

Think of a favorite sport. Who invented it? When and where were its first games held? Sometimes these questions cannot be answered because some sports developed over many years, or even centuries. The ideas and rules behind other sports, however, were clearly created by one person or several people at a specific point in time.

This book describes ten pairs of sports. Read about each pair and guess which one came first. Then turn the page for the answer.

▲ **Philippides ran from the city of Marathon, Greece, to the city of Athens in 490 B.C. The Olympic Marathon event, a race that covers 26.2 miles (42.16 km), is named after his run.**

Turn the page to
find out which
came first.

# Which Came First?

## Football

Although it's called football, kicking is not the main way the ball gets moved in this game. Only two players, the kicker and the punter, are allowed to move the ball with their feet.

▲ **Green Bay Packers' Brett Favre in 2005**

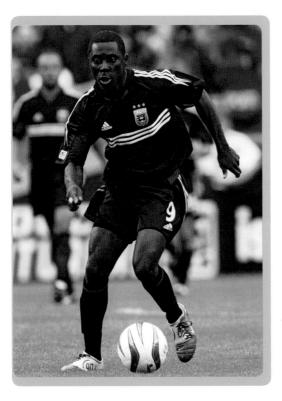

## Soccer

Millions of people in more than 200 countries play soccer. The United States, however, is the only place where the sport is called *soccer*. People in other countries call it football.

◀ **Fourteen-year-old soccer sensation
Freddy Adu in 2004**

# Answer: Soccer

Games resembling soccer have been played for at least 3,000 years. Modern soccer, however, was invented in England in the mid-1800s. Several schools set up the first rules for the game in 1848.

American football comes from two sports, soccer and **rugby**. In 1879, a college student named Walter Camp began to develop the rules that led to today's game.

▲ **English soccer great David Beckham in a 2005 game against Colombia**

Footballs are often referred to as "pigskins." This name is misleading, however, because footballs are made of leather from cows.

Turn the page to find out which came first.

# Which Came First?

Pedro Martinez of the New York Mets in a 2005 game against the Florida Marlins

## Baseball

Often referred to as America's national pastime, baseball's popularity has spread around the world. Outside the United States, baseball is particularly popular in East Asia and Latin America.

## Softball

Softball is popular in both the **fast-pitch** and **slow-pitch** forms. Today, softball is played in more than 85 countries and is especially popular among young women.

Jennie Finch, U.S. Olympic Softball ▷ Team pitcher, in 2004

7

# Answer: Baseball

People have been playing baseball since the early 1800s. It came from two English games, called **cricket** and **rounders**. In 1845, a New Yorker named Alexander Cartwright wrote the rules on which the modern game is based.

In 1887, George Hancock invented softball in Chicago. People could play this form of indoor baseball when the weather was too cold to play outside.

The first softball game was played using a broom handle for a bat and a folded boxing glove as a ball.

◄ **Derek Jeter of the New York Yankees in a 2005 game against the Boston Red Sox**

Turn the page to
find out which
came first.

# Which Came First?

## Basketball

Players who are
tall have an advantage
in basketball because
they are closer to the
basket's rim. Basketball
is the world's most
popular indoor sport.

▲ **Michael Jordan of the Chicago Bulls in the
1997 NBA Finals**

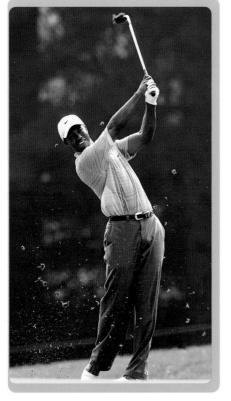

## Golf

The average golf ball
has around 400 dimples on
its surface. When the ball
is struck, these dimples
allow it to travel twice the
distance of a smooth ball.

◀ **Tiger Woods at the PGA Championship in 2005**

9

# Answer: Golf

The first game of golf was played in Scotland in the 1400s. The earliest golfers used pebbles as balls and sticks for clubs.

A teacher in Massachusetts named James Naismith invented basketball in 1891. He needed a game that rowdy kids could play indoors during the cold winter months. A soccer ball and a peach-basket hoop were used in the first game.

◀ Fifteen-year-old Michelle Wie at the U.S. Women's Open in 2004

The first golf balls were made of horse or cow leather wrapped around feathers. They did not travel very far.

# Which Came First?

## Tennis

Tennis can be played on grass, clay, or concrete courts. Professionals compete in four major international events, called **Grand Slam** tournaments. Wimbledon, held every summer in England, is the oldest and most famous of these tournaments.

◄ **Serena Williams playing in the 2005 U.S. Open, a Grand Slam tournament**

## Volleyball

There are two versions of volleyball, indoor and beach. Beach volleyball is played on sand, while the indoor game is played in a gym.

**Kerri Walsh at the** ▶ **2004 Summer Olympic Games**

# Answer: Tennis

Modern tennis is based on a game played in France in the 1300s. Major Walter Wingfield, an English inventor of games, published the first book of tennis rules in 1873. Wingfield designed the game for guests he'd invited to his home for a garden party.

A Massachusetts teacher named William Morgan invented volleyball for his class in 1895. He combined aspects of tennis and **handball** in creating the new game.

◀ **Superstar Andre Agassi in 2004**

Tennis balls used to be white. In 1972, yellow balls were introduced after research showed that TV viewers could see them more easily than balls of other colors.

# Which Came First?

Turn the page to find out which came first.

### Ice Hockey

In North America, this game is known simply as hockey. It used to be played on frozen ponds until the invention of artificial ice rinks.

▲ **Lake Placid Olympics, 1980**

### Lacrosse

In lacrosse, players use sticks with nets attached to the ends to throw a ball into the other team's goal. The playing area is slightly bigger than a football field.

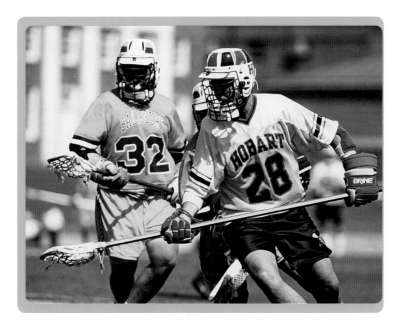

▲ **A lacrosse championship game in Maryland in 1994**

# Answer: Lacrosse

Native Americans invented lacrosse as early as the 1400s. In the early days of this game, hundreds of people played at a time and the field could be miles (kms) long. Some games would even last for days!

Ice hockey was invented in the mid-1800s in Canada. In 1875, modern ice hockey rules were written and the first indoor game was played in Montreal.

The sticks used in this Native American game reminded French explorers of a Bishop's staff, which in French is called *la crosse.* The French words *la crosse* became lacrosse in English.

Turn the page to
find out which
came first.

# Which Came First?

## Track and Field

The events in track and field test people's strength, speed, and endurance. Track events focus on running, while field events test jumping and throwing skills.

◀ **Jackie Joyner-Kersee at the 1992 Olympic Games**

## Swimming

Speed and endurance are also important in swimming. Competitive swimmers try to cover a set distance in as little time as possible.

**Olympic gold medal winner ▶ Michael Phelps of the USA competing at the Swimming World Championships in 2005**

# Answer: Track and Field

A cook named Koroibos won the first foot race in 776 B.C. The contest took place at the first Olympics in ancient Greece. The track, called the **stadion**, was 600 feet (183 m) long.

Swimming as a modern sport began in England when the National Swimming Society held contests in 1837. Most of the contestants used a swimming style called the breaststroke.

◀ **High school student Jesse Owens in 1932, before he became a winner of four gold medals at the 1936 Olympics**

Swimming events at the 1896 Olympics in Athens, Greece, took place in the open sea, not in pools!

Turn the page to
find out which
came first.

# Which Came First?

▲ **Skateboard champ Tony Hawk in 2004**

## Skateboarding

When the first boards were made, skateboarding was called sidewalk surfing. Once used simply for recreation or to get around town, skateboarding has turned into a competitive **extreme sport**.

## Figure Skating

Athletes perform routines of leaps, spins, and glides during a figure-skating competition. Judges choose winners by rating each participant's performance.

**Michelle Kwan, at the** ▶
**U.S. Figure Skating**
**Championships in 2005**

**17**

# Answer: Figure Skating

People have ice skated for hundreds of years, but figure skating was only invented in the 1850s. The first World Championship was held in 1896.

The first modern skateboard was made in a California surf shop in 1958. The first skateboard competition was held in 1963. In the 1970s, the creation of **skate parks** and better skateboards led to modern skateboarding.

The blades of the first ice skates were made from animal bones. People tied the skates to their feet with leather straps.

◀ **U.S. gold medal winner Sarah Hughes at the 2002 Winter Olympics**

Turn the page to find out which came first.

# Which Came First?

## Super Bowl

The National Football League (NFL) is made up of two **conferences**, the American and the National. Each winter, the winners from each conference play each other in the Super Bowl to determine the NFL champion.

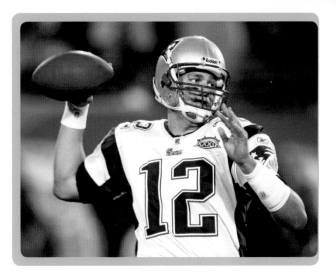

▲ **New England Patriots' quarterback Tom Brady at the 2005 Super Bowl**

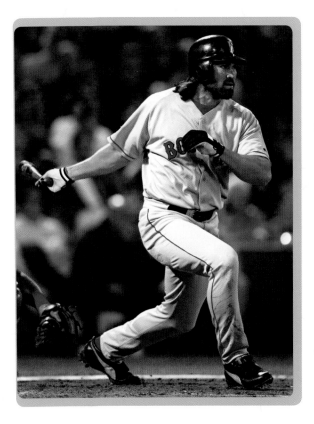

## World Series

Major League Baseball has two **leagues**, the American and the National. Every October, the winning team from each league plays in the World Series. The first team to win four games is the champion.

◄ **Johnny Damon of the Boston Red Sox, during a 2004 World Series game**

19

# Answer: World Series

In 1903, the American League's Boston Red Sox defeated the National League's Pittsburgh Pirates in the first World Series. The games were held to build better relations between the two rival leagues.

When the Green Bay Packers defeated the Kansas City Chiefs in 1967, they became the first Super Bowl champions. Today the Super Bowl is broadcast in 182 countries.

The name Super Bowl came from the Kansas City Chiefs' owner, who thought of it after watching his daughter play with a toy called the Super Ball.

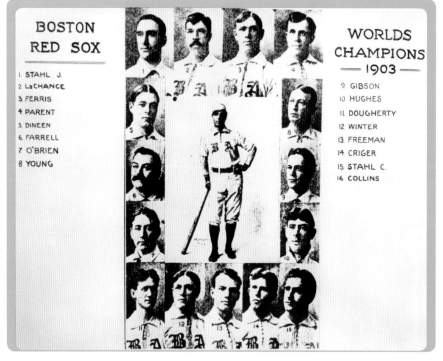

▲ Poster from the 1903 World Series

# Which Came First?

## Olympics

The Olympics are held every two years, alternating between summer and winter games. The best athletes in the world compete in these events, which were begun to promote world peace.

▲ **Hollie Vise, U.S. Olympic Team Trials, 2004**

## X-Games

Held every summer and winter, the X-Games showcase extreme sports. Just as in the Olympics, participants win **gold**, **silver**, or **bronze medals** for placing first, second, or third in their sport's competition.

Summer events include various skateboard, motocross, and other competitions. At the winter games, competitors participate in snowboarding, ice sliding, and other challenges.

◄ **Izumi Amaike at the 2005 Winter X-Games**

# Answer: Olympics

Ancient Greece was the site of the first Olympics in 776 B.C. The games continued until A.D. 393. The original games were a religious festival to honor the Greek god Zeus. The modern Olympics started in A.D. 1896.

The first X-Games were held in 1995. The Winter X-Games were added in 1997 and were televised in 198 different countries and territories.

1896 Olympic ▶
Games in
Athens, Greece

The first Olympics were held every four years for 12 centuries in the Greek town of Olympia.

Turn the page to
find out which
came first.

# Which Came First?

## Tour de France

Held every July in France, the Tour de France is a bicycle race that covers more than 2,000 miles (3,219 km). With as many as 200 cyclists competing, it is the largest annual professional sporting event in the world.

◀ **Lance Armstrong riding to his seventh win in the 2005 Tour de France**

## World Cup

Countries compete every four years for the title of world champion in soccer's World Cup. Separate tournaments are held for men's and women's teams.

◀ **Oguchi Onyewu (#22) of the USA and Ramon Morales (#11) of Mexico during the 2006 World Cup qualification games**

# Answer: Tour de France

The French newspaper *L'Auto* started the Tour de France in 1903 as a publicity stunt. The Tour was started to compete with another bike race that was sponsored by a rival newspaper.

The World Cup soccer game is watched by more people than any other sporting event in the world. The men's tournament was first held in 1930. The first women's World Cup was held in 1991.

During the three weeks of the Tour de France, the cyclist who holds the overall lead wears a yellow jersey while racing.

# Which Comes Next?

Here are two sports that may be taking off. Which one do you think will become popular first?

## Kiteboarding

A large kite is used to pull a person on a board across water. This sport is similar to wakeboarding and windsurfing. In wakeboarding, however, a boat pulls the board. In windsurfing, a sail catches the wind to move the board.

▲ **Kiteboarder in Hawaii**

## All-Terrain Boarding (ATB)

This sport was developed for snowboarders who wanted an activity during the warm months. ATB, sometimes called mountainboarding, is now its own sport. A mountain board is similar to an oversized skateboard. People can compete in races and **freestyle events**.

◄ **Mountainboarder in Death Valley, California**

# Scorecard

How many did you get correct?

| Which Came First? | Answer |
|---|---|
| Football or Soccer | |
| Baseball or Softball | |
| Basketball or Golf | |
| Tennis or Volleyball | |
| Ice Hockey or Lacrosse | |
| Track and Field or Swimming | |
| Skateboarding or Figure Skating | |
| Super Bowl or World Series | |
| Olympics or X-Games | |
| Tour de France or World Cup | |

# Bonus Questions

Now you know which of the sporting events in this book came first. Here are a few bonus questions.

1. **Hicham El Guerrouj holds the world record for running the fastest mile. He ran it in a time of**
   a. 2:56 minutes
   c. 5:13 minutes
   b. 3:43 minutes
   d. 7:01 minutes

2. **Which sport has the highest yearly attendance in the United States?**
   a. basketball
   c. football
   b. baseball
   d. ice hockey

3. **In 1962, Philadelphia's Wilt Chamberlain set the record for most points scored in an NBA game. How many points did he score?**
   a. 30
   b. 47
   c. 75
   d. 100

4. **What country has won five World Cups, the highest total of any country?**
   a. Brazil
   c. United Kingdom (England)
   b. United States of America
   d. Italy

## Just the Facts

- Women were excluded from early Olympic contests, so they started their own games. They called them the Games of Hera, after the Greek goddess of women and Earth.
- Golf quickly became very popular when it was invented in Scotland. In 1457, the Scottish government made golf illegal so that people wouldn't waste all their time playing.
- Nine of the ten most-watched programs in television history are Super Bowls.
- The Special Olympics is a competition for kids and adults with learning or physical disabilities. The event is modeled after the Olympic Games.
- In England, soccer is often referred to as "association football." The name *soccer* is a slang term that comes from the word *association*.
- Major League Baseball attracts more than 50 million people to its ballparks each year. That number is almost equal to attendance at all other American professional sporting events combined.
- There are around 15,000 golf courses in the United States for the 24 million people who play golf at least once a year.
- Track and field has two seasons. Outdoor track takes place during the summer. Indoor track takes place in the winter and uses a smaller track.

# The History of Sporting Events

**776 B.C.** First Olympics; First track and field event

**1400s** Golf and lacrosse invented

**1837** First swimming competition

**1845** Rules of baseball written

**1848** Rules of soccer written

**1873** Rules of tennis written

**1875** First organized indoor hockey game

**1879** Rules of football written

**1887** Softball invented

**1891** Basketball invented

**1895** Volleyball invented

**1896** First modern Olympics;
First World Figure Skating Championships

**1903** First Tour de France;
First World Series

**1930** First men's World Cup

**1963** First skateboard competition

**1967** First Super Bowl

**1991** First women's World Cup

**1995** First X-Games competition

**1997** First Winter X-Games competition

# Glossary

**bronze medal** (BRONZ MED-uhl)   medal awarded to the third-place finisher at both the modern Olympics and the X-Games

**conferences** (KON-fur-uhnss-uhz)   groups of sports teams that compete mainly with one another

**cricket** (KRIK-it)   an outdoor game, popular in England, that uses a flat bat and a ball

**extreme sport** (ek-STREEM SPORT)   a new, nontraditional sport that combines skill with an element of risk

**fast-pitch** (FAST-PICH)   form of softball in which the pitcher throws the ball underhand at a fast speed

**freestyle events** (FREE-stile i-VENTS)   extreme-sports events in which participants compete by performing tricks and special moves

**gold medal** (GOHLD MED-uhl)   medal awarded to the first-place finisher at both the modern Olympics and the X-Games

**Grand Slam** (GRAND SLAM)   the four major tournaments in tennis: the Australian Open, the French Open, Wimbledon, and the U.S. Open

**handball** (HAND-*bawl*)   a game where players hit a ball against a wall with their hands

**leagues** (LEEGZ)   groups of teams; teams within a league mainly compete with one another

**rounders** (ROUN-duhrz)   an English game that resembles baseball

**rugby** (RUHG-bee)   a game similar to American football in which players kick, pass, and carry an oval ball

**silver medal** (SIL-vur MED-uhl)   medal awarded to the second-place finisher at both the modern Olympics and the X-Games

**skate parks** (SKAYT PARKS)   places for skateboarders to perform tricks

**slow-pitch** (SLOH-PICH)   a form of softball in which the pitcher throws the ball underhand at a slow speed with a significant arc

**stadion** (STAY-dee-on)   a track at the first Olympics that covered 600 feet (183 m)

## Bibliography

**Gorn, Elliott J., and Warren J. Goldstein**. *A Brief History of American Sports*. Champaign, IL: University of Illinois Press (2004).

**Herzog, Brad**. *The Sports 100: The One Hundred Most Important People in American Sports History*. New York: Macmillan General Reference (1996).

**www.inventors.about.com**

**www.museum.upenn.edu**

**www.tennisgifts.com/info.htm**

**www.wikipedia.org/wiki/Main_Page**

**www.worldalmanacforkids.com/**

## Read More

**Barrett, Norman**. *Sports Facts*. New York: DK Children (1996).

**Jones, Mary Varilla, ed**. *Sports Illustrated for Kids: Year in Sports 2006*. New York: Scholastic Reference (2005).

**Ritter, Lawrence S**. *Leagues Apart: The Men and Times of the Negro Baseball Leagues*. New York: HarperTrophy (1999).

## Learn More Online

Visit these Web sites to learn more about sporting events:

**expn.go.com/expn/index**

**www.funtrivia.com/quizzes/for_children/topics_for_kids/sports_for_kids.html**

**www.sikids.com**

**www.timelineindex.com/content/select/382/912,693,382**

# Index

Adu, Freddy  5
Agassi, Andre  12
all-terrain boarding  25
Amaike, Izumi  21
American League  19, 20
Armstrong, Lance  23

baseball  7, 8, 19, 20, 26, 27, 28, 29
basketball  9, 10, 26, 27, 29
Beckham, David  6
Brady, Tom  19

Camp, Walter  6
Cartwright, Alexander  8
Chamberlain, Wilt  27

Damon, Johnny  19

El Guerrouj, Hicham  27

Favre, Brett  5
figure skating  17, 18, 26, 29
Finch, Jennie  7
football  5, 6, 13, 19, 20, 26, 27, 28, 29

golf  9, 10, 26, 28, 29

Hancock, George  8
Hawk, Tony  17
Hughes, Sarah  18

ice hockey  13, 14, 26, 27, 29
ice sliding  21

Jeter, Derek  8
Jordan, Michael  9
Joyner-Kersee, Jackie  15

kiteboarding  25
Koroibos  16
Kwan, Michelle  17

lacrosse  13, 14, 26, 29

Major League Baseball  19, 28
Marathon  4
Martinez, Pedro  7
Morales, Ramon  23
Morgan, William  12
motocross  21
mountain-boarding  25

Naismith, James  10
National Football League  19
National League  19, 20

Olympics  4, 11, 13, 15, 16, 18, 21, 22, 26, 28, 29
Onyewu, Oguchi  23
Owens, Jesse  16

Phelps, Michael  15

skateboarding  17, 18, 25, 26, 29

snowboarding  21, 25
soccer  5, 6, 10, 23, 24, 26, 28, 29
softball  7, 8, 26, 29
Super Bowl  19, 20, 26, 28, 29
swimming  15, 16, 26, 29

tennis  11, 12, 26, 29
Tour de France  23, 24, 26, 29
track and field  15, 16, 26, 28, 29

Vise, Hollie  21
volleyball  11, 12, 26, 29

wakeboarding  25
Walsh, Kerri  11
Wie, Michelle  10
Williams, Serena  11
Wimbledon  11
windsurfing  25
Wingfield, Major Walter  12
Woods, Tiger  9
World Cup  23, 24, 26, 27, 29
World Series  19, 20, 26, 29

X-Games  21, 22, 26, 29

Zeus  22

## About the Author

Gabriel Kaufman works in children's publishing and enjoys watching and playing sports in his free time. While growing up in Illinois, his favorite sports teams were the Chicago Cubs and Bulls. He currently lives in Brooklyn, New York.